Editors
Karen Tam Froloff
Gisela Lee

Managing Editor
Karen J. Goldfluss, M.S. Ed.

Editor-in-Chief
Sharon Coan, M.S. Ed.

Cover Artist
Jessica Orlando

Art Coordinator
Kevin Barnes

Creative Director
Wendy Froshay

Imaging
Rosa C. See

Product Manager
Phil Garcia

Publisher
Mary D. Smith, M.S. Ed.

How to

Word Problems

Grades 5–6

Author

Kathleen M. Kopp, M.S. Ed.

Teacher Created Resources, Inc.
6421 Industry Way
Westminster, CA 92683
www.teachercreated.com

ISBN: 978-1-57690-950-8

©2002 Teacher Created Resources, Inc.
Reprinted, 2007
Made in U.S.A.

Table of Contents

How to ••••••••••••••••••••• Use This Book

A Note to Teachers and Parents

Welcome to the "How to" math series! You have chosen one of two dozen books designed to give students the information and practice they need to acquire important concepts in specific areas of math. The goal of the "How to" math books is to give children an extra boost as they work toward mastery of the math skills established by the National Council of Teacher of Mathematics (NCTM) and outlined in grade-level scope and sequence guidelines.

The design of this book allows teachers or parents to use it for a variety of purposes and needs. Each of the units contains one "How to" page and three practice pages. The "How to" section of each unit precedes the practice pages and provides needed information such as a concept or math rule review, important terms and formulas to remember, or step-by-step guidelines necessary for using the practice pages. While most "How to" pages are written for direct use by students, in some lower-grade level books, these pages are presented as instructional pages or direct lessons to be used by a teacher or parent prior to introducing the practice pages.

About This Book

How to Solve Word Problems: Grades 5 and 6 allows students to utilize their computational, estimating, and thinking skills in a variety of believable, natural situations. Each word problem is genuine and could arise at any time in a child's life or in the lives of adults he or she knows. This quality of authenticity draws learners into the world of mathematical word problems.

The activities in this book will help students learn important new skills or reinforce skills already learned in the following areas:

- identifying and applying problem-solving strategies
- identifying and applying patterns to problem-solving situations
- analyzing situations to determine the best course of action
- comparing quantities
- calculating solutions
- estimating to determine a likely solution
- applying linear, volume and capacity, weight and mass, and time measurement skills
- identifying fractional quantities through fractional computations
- applying geometry skills
- applying algebraic thinking skills, including the formulation of equations
- collecting, organizing, and analyzing data to synthesize word problems

Regardless of their ability to add and subtract and multiply and divide, students may complete the practice pages following the concepts presented on the "How to" pages with ease. Students may require the use of a calculator when working with higher numbers or if their multiplication and other computation skills are in need of remediation.

Once having completed this book, students will feel ready to take on whatever mathematical problems arise in daily life!

How to Solve Word Problems: Grades 5 and 6 matches a number of NCTM standards, including these main topics and specific features:

Problem Solving

The activities in this book offer a wide array of open-ended, real-world problems for which students must use their mathematical expertise to provide solutions. As part of the problem-solving process, students meaningfully apply their problem-solving skills to verify and interpret results and justify decisions based on these results.

Reasoning

The activities in this book enlist students' reasoning skills as part of the problem-solving process. They must reason to apply the best problem-solving strategy as well as to work through each individual situation.

Computation and Estimation

The activities in this book require students to compute and estimate results with whole numbers, fractions, and decimals. This includes computation and estimation in isolation as well as in the solution of real-world situations.

Patterns and Functions

Some of the activities in this book offer specific situations in which students must identify and apply a mathematical pattern or rule to represent and solve problems. The most frequent application is presented with a T-chart in which students must analyze the relationship between two variables, apply the algebraic equation, or identify and apply the function to determine additional outcomes.

Algebra

Some of the activities in this book encourage the development and understanding of variables and algebraic equations. Through the problem-solving process, students also use a variety of methods to solve linear equations.

Other Standards

The activities in this book provide a range of additional skill applications such as mathematical communication, connections to other subject areas and to the world outside the classroom, the development and understanding of geometric objects and relationships, and the use of geometry to solve problems.

1 How to ••••• Apply Problem-Solving Strategies

Facts to Know

Knowing how to apply the four-step plan will help solve word problems.

Four-Step Plan

1. **Read and Understand the Problem.**

   Trying to solve a problem without understanding it would be like jumping into the deep end of a pool without knowing how to swim. Ask yourself these questions to help understand the problem better:

   • Why is this problem important?

   • What do I need to find out?

   • What information do I know?

   • Do I have all the information I need to solve it?

2. **Make a Plan.**

   Consider the plan your swimming lesson. After you decide what you need to find out, decide how to go about discovering the answer. Some valuable problem-solving strategies include the following:

   — acting it out

   — drawing a picture

   — looking for a pattern

   — guessing and checking

   — working backward

   — making a list

   — making a table or chart

   — using logical reasoning

3. **Solve the Problem.**

   Now you can jump into the pool and put those swimming lessons to use. Use the strategy you think best to solve the problem. Then find the answer.

4. **Check to Be Sure Your Answer Makes Sense.**

   If you've applied your lessons correctly, you're swimming by now. Check your answer. Does it make sense? Check to make sure your answer is not unreasonable. Estimation is an important skill. If you expected the answer to be about 400 and you come up with 2,000, chances are you did something wrong.

   Also, be sure you answered the question that was asked. If a problem asks you to identify the fruit you are most likely to randomly select from a bowl, the answer isn't 32 or 5/9, it's perhaps "an apple" or "a banana."

   Refer to this four-step plan with each word problem you encounter in this book. If you do, you'll be ready to swim through the challenge of solving word problems without any assistance!

Directions: Read each word problem. Use what you learned on page 5 to answer the questions about each problem.

A dairy farmer has determined that his fence needs to be replaced along one side. He knows how much he is able to spend on the fencing supplies.

1. What information does the farmer need to know before he shops for replacement items? _____

   _____

2. Let's say the farmer discovers he needs to replace 50 posts and 75 boards. The estimated cost of these supplies is $1,200. What does the farmer need to compare this to? _____

   _____

Lynne has four times as many pencils as Erin. Erin has half as many pencils as Sue. Falon has three times as many pencils as Erin. How many pencils does each girl have?

5. What do you need to know before you answer this problem?

   _____

6. Would knowing how many pencils the girls have in total enable you to figure out the answer? If so, how?

   _____

   _____

You wish to help your parents shop for a new refrigerator. They are not sure whether to get one that measures 18, 19, 21, or 24 cubic feet. They do know that they want to get the largest one they can afford for the best price and value. The dimensions of the space for the refrigerator are 34 inches wide by 33 inches deep by 70 inches high.

3. What information is important when you go to the appliance store?

   _____

4. How can you help your parents determine the best cost per size?

   _____

   _____

Aaron wants to take a trip. He really wants to go to Washington, D.C. He has almost $1,000 saved for this trip. He wants to arrive quickly so that he has more time to enjoy the sights.

7. Once Aaron has researched all of the transportation expenses (e.g., plane, train, car rental, bus, driving, etc.), what should he consider next?

   _____

8. If Aaron discovers that flying will cost over $800, should he choose that method of transportation? Explain.

   _____

   _____

1 ▶ Practice ••••••• Applying a Problem-Solving Plan

Directions: Use what you learned on page 5 about making a plan and solving the problem to find the answer to these word problems.

1. Hal earns the following amounts for each weekly chore.

   Which chores can he do to earn . . .

Hal's Weekly Chore List			
take out trash	$1.00	dust the furniture	$1.00
do the dishes	$1.00	clean the garage	$2.00
make his bed	$1.00	clean his room	$1.00
sweep the floors	$1.00	water the plants	$1.00
mow the lawn	$10.00	vacuum the floor	$3.00

   $5.00? _____

   $10.00? _____

   $15.00? _____

   $20.00? _____

2. A box has a volume of 560 inches. The width of the box is 7 inches. Find out how long and high the box is. (**Hint:** *volume = length x width x height*) _____

3. Mr. Martin has 30 students in his class. He has four more girls than boys. How many boys and girls are in Mr. Martin's class? _____

4. The temperature so far this week has been 85° F, 87° F, and 90° F. What would the temperature have to be tomorrow for the average weekly temperature to be 86° F? (**Hint:** To find the average, add the numbers and divide by the total addends. See page 13.) _____

5. While building their pool, the Eriksons have three tile colors, three deck colors, and five fill colors to choose from. How many different combinations may they select from to complete their pool? _____

6. What prime number, when first multiplied by 7, then added to 7, then divided by 2, equals 21? (**Hint:** Prime numbers have only 1 and themselves as factors. See page 9.)

   _____

7. Marla has 32 items of jewelry she made to sell at the flea market. She wants to display her wares in rows containing the same number of items. How many different ways might she arrange them? _____

8. John's mom makes spaghetti for dinner every 8 days. They eat hot dogs every 12 days. After how many days will the family have to decide between hot dogs and spaghetti?

   _____

1 ▶ Practice • • • • • Checking for Reasonable Answers

Directions: Use what you learned on page 5 about checking to be sure your answer makes sense with the following questions. Circle *yes* or *no* and then give an explanation for your reasoning.

1. Dirk's family spent $200 on food, $280 on lodging, $150 on sightseeing, and $80 on gas. When asked to calculate how much the family spent on their vacation, Dirk answered, "$1,000." Does his answer make sense?   **Yes   No**

   Explain:_____

2. Ben lives in a small town of about 1,000 people. The town covers about 50 square miles of land. Reading the local paper, Ben sees that the mayor has estimated that about 200 people live in each square mile.

   Should Ben question the mayor's mathematics?   **Yes   No**

   Explain:_____

3. A box of cookies usually sells for $1.35. Today they are on sale at two boxes for $3.00. Is this really a deal?   **Yes   No**

   Explain:_____

4. Some students decide to work together to sell a total of 2,000 tickets for a school raffle. Each person wishes to sell about 200 tickets. The group decides they need at least 10 people. Is this a reasonable number of students?   **Yes   No**

   Explain:_____

5. Mr. Jackson's train averages about 30 miles per hour, factoring in all of the stops. He lives about 20 miles from work and estimates his daily commute to be about 45 minutes each way. Is he about right?   **Yes   No**

   Explain:_____

6. The school drama team, consisting of 40 participants, needs to arrange for transportation when they perform outside their school. They figure that 5 cars are needed to make the trek. Will this do?   **Yes   No**

   Explain:_____

7. Your little sister tells you she has $14.31 stashed away in a safe place. You estimate this to be about $25 less than what you have. When you count your secret holdings, you discover you have $43.55. Was your estimate way off?   **Yes   No**

   Explain:_____

8. Because she doesn't have time to bake, Tim's mom decides to buy cupcakes for his birthday to send to school. She guesses she'll need to spend no more than $10 to cover a class of 33. The cupcakes come in half-dozen packages at $2.59 per package. Was Tim's mom's estimate correct? **(Hint:** one dozen = 12)   **Yes   No**

   Explain:_____

Facts to Know

Look for the key word(s) when deciding whether to add, subtract, multiply, or divide to solve word problems.

Add	Subtract	Multiply	Divide
total	how much less	each (building	each (separating
in all	less . . . than	larger groups)	into smaller groups)
altogether	how many fewer	groups of	divide by
sum	. . . left	product	shared or divided
entire	difference	percent (of)	evenly
tally	minus	. . . of	quotient
how many more			
more . . . than			

Kinds of Numbers

Remember that *even numbers* are always divisible by 2. *Odd numbers*, when separated into two equal groups, have one remaining.

Remember *place value*:

millions	hundred thousands	ten thousands	thousands	hundreds	tens	ones
6	8	0	9	3	5	2

The number in the chart above has 3 hundreds, 2 ones, and 0 ten thousands, etc.

A *multiple* is a number you multiply several times. A *factor* is a number that divides evenly into a larger number.

> **Example:** Multiples of 3 = 3, 6, 9, 12, 15, 18 . . .
>
> Factors of 10 = 1, 2, 5, and 10

Prime numbers are numbers that are divisible only by 1 and themselves. *Composite* numbers have more factors than just 1 and themselves.

> **Example:** 3, 7, and 23 are prime. They are only divisible by 1 and themselves.
>
> 8, 12, and 30 are composite. They each have several factors.

Looking for *patterns* in numbers can help you identify answers.

> **Example:** Roger builds a block house by adding two blocks each time. How many blocks will his tower have after five additions?

Additions	1	2	3	4	5
Total Blocks	2	4	6	8	10

The number of blocks is 2 times the number of additions. On his 100th addition he will have 200 blocks.

2 Practice ·············· Determining the Operation to Solve Word Problems

Directions: Use the information on page 9 about key words to decide whether to add, subtract, multiply, or divide. Then solve each of these word problems.

1. Roger sees a sale on a video game he's been wanting. Gary's Games runs an ad for $26.98. Roger has $23.25 saved. How much more money does he need to buy the game? _____

2. Amy gets party favors that cost $1.89 each with tax. How much will she spend if she invites 5 friends to her party? _____

3. Angel can get 3 games at Fred's Fun Village for $27. How much does each game cost? _____

4. Les empties his piggy bank to find $114.56. If he had put the same amount in each week for 8 weeks, how much were his weekly savings? _____

5. The votes are in! Each grade level was asked to vote for its favorite school lunch. Tally the results to see what the students prefer to have served for school lunch.

Favorite School Lunch	3rd grade	4th grade	5th grade	6th grade	Total
Hamburger	26	28	15	21	
Pizza	32	40	44	26	
Taco	30	15	30	14	
Spaghetti	25	32	33	60	

Favorite school lunch _____

6. At a local movie theater, the manager tallied 365 patrons who came to see "Blast of the Beast" over the weekend. He counted 411 who came to see "T-Rex Terrors." How many more patrons saw "T-Rex Terrors" than "Blast of the Beast"? _____

7. An average medium pepperoni pizza at Pizza-o-rama has 15 slices of pepperoni on it. If the restaurant sold 57 medium pepperoni pizzas one Friday night, about how many slices of pepperoni did they sell? _____

8. You and your friends are stamp collectors. When you compare collections, you find that you own 132 stamps, one friend has 211 stamps, and a second friend has 199 stamps. How many stamps do you and your friends have in all? _____

Directions: Use the information on page 9 about different kinds of numbers to answer the following questions.

An arena has 10 sections, each labeled with letters A through J. Each section has 500 seats. How many seats . . .

1. are even numbered? _____

2. are odd numbered? _____

3. are a multiple of 10? _____

4. have a 5 in the tens digit? _____

5. have a 3 in the hundreds digit? _____

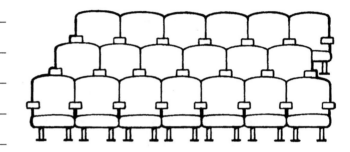

Looking at the list of colored candies in a package of candy, you wish to share all the colors evenly among five friends and yourself.

6. Which colors can you share without leftover pieces? _____

7. What if you were sharing with just one friend? List how many of each color you and your friend would receive.

blue _____ green _____ yellow _____

orange _____ red _____ brown _____

Each hallway has 10 sections of 36 lockers.

8. How many of the first lockers numbered 1 through 36 are prime-numbered lockers? _____

9. How many of them are composite-numbered lockers? _____

10. If you know your locker is in the first section, are you more or less likely to receive an even- or odd-numbered locker? Explain your answer. _____

_____

Dogs run a track for exercise. Barkley crosses the starting point every 6 minutes, Pal every 4 minutes, and Spot every 8 minutes.

11. How many minutes will it take for all of these dogs to cross at the same time? _____

2 ▶ Practice •••••••••• Using Patterns to Solve Numerical Word Problems

Directions: Use the information on page 9 about using patterns to complete the charts and solve these word problems.

Ajax Shipping packs up to 1,000 items per delivery. If they wish to pack boxes with between 25 and 200 items with none left over, how many ways might they pack a full load? List the number of boxes and the number of items in each box for each way.

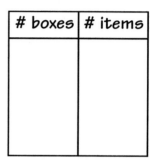

# boxes	# items

1. Number of ways they may pack _____

Jessica's baby brother weighed 11 pounds when he was 3 months old, 13 pounds when he was 6 months old, and 15 pounds when he was 9 months old. If this pattern continues, how much will he weigh when he is . . .

2. 18 months old? _____

3. 2 years old? _____

age in months				
weight in pounds				

Rollover	Amount
	$1,000,000

A lotto jackpot doubles (rolls over) each time no one wins. If the jackpot starts at $1,000,000 . . .

4. how much will it be worth after three rollovers?

   _____

5. how much will it be worth after five rollovers?

   _____

Lonny starts with two blocks. He builds a tower by adding two times the previous number of blocks with each addition.

addition	0	1	2			
# of blocks	2	4	8			

6. How many blocks will his tower have after five additions? _____

Facts to Know

Sometimes a problem is best solved by estimating the answer instead of finding the exact answer.

> ### Example
>
> Hector wishes to figure out how much his baseball collection is worth. By checking some Internet resources, he discovers he has two cards worth $25.15 each, four worth $14.75 each, and the remaining 10 are worth between $3.00 and $5.00 each. Help Hector determine how much his collection is worth.

Estimate by Rounding or Using Front Ends

You can estimate by rounding each of Hector's figures to the nearest dollar or by using the numerical values from the front end, the place values farthest to the left. In this case, these are the values of the tens and ones digits. Start with the two most expensive cards.

Step 1: Estimate	**Step 2:** Multiply	**Step 3:** Add
$25.15 ⟶ $25.00	$25 x 2 = $50	$50
$14.75 ⟶ $15.00	$15 x 4 = $60	+ $60
		$110

Hint: Estimate with multiples of 5 when multiplying.

Estimate by Averaging

Then assume each of the remaining 10 cards to be worth the average of the range. To find the average, add the totals ($5 and $3) and divide by the number of addends (2).

$3.00 + $5.00 = $8.00 $8.00 ÷ 2 = $4.00

Hector has 10 cards worth about $4.00 each. Multiply to find this total.

$4.00 x 10 = $40.00

Add this total to the one above, and you have an estimation of how much Hector's baseball cards are worth.

$110.00 + $40.00 = $150.00

By using the estimation process, you can tell Hector that his collection is worth about $150.00.

3 ▶Practice ••••••••••• Applying Estimation Skills to Solve Word Problems

Directions: Use what you learned on page 13 to estimate the following answers.

1. Roger's automobile uses one gallon of gas for every 30 miles he drives on the highway. If Roger's car has a 15-gallon tank, about how far can he go on one tank of gas if he does mostly highway driving? _____

2. Roger's car gets 25 miles to the gallon during city driving. About how far can Roger drive on one tank if he does mostly city driving? _____

3. About how much farther can Roger drive on one tank of gas if he drives mostly on the highway than if he were to drive mostly in the city? _____

4. Betsy calculated her mileage on a weekly basis. Her calculations are in the table below.

week #	1	2	3	4	5	6	7	8
miles per gallon	26	28	29	28	27	28	25	27

Estimate the average miles per gallon Betsy got over the eight weeks. _____

Betsy has a 13-gallon tank. About how many miles could Betsy travel each week before needing to fill up her tank? _____

5. The whole fifth grade is going on a trip. The class has 126 students. If the park requires that every five students be supervised by at least one chaperone, about how many chaperones are needed for the trip? _____

6. Eight hundred eleven people audition for a new play. If the play's producers could hold 70 auditions each day, about how many days will they need to audition everyone?

_____

7. A recent poll shows that the lead candidate would receive 1,301 votes, and his opponent 962 votes. If the election were held today, estimate the number of votes the leader would win by. _____

8. Using the figures from number 7 above, about how many people were polled?

_____

9. A factory produces about 300,000 potato chips per day. If about 100 chips go in each bag, how many bags do they produce daily? _____ weekly (in a five-day work-week)? _____

10. The local vet sees between 12 to 16 dogs, 10 to 12 cats, and 16 to 20 other miscellaneous pets each day. About how many animals does she see daily? _____ weekly (in a five-day work-week)? _____

3 ▶ Practice ...... Estimating Money Word Problems

Directions: Use what you learned on page 13 about rounding and front-end estimation to solve the following word problems that deal with money.

Jean's parents have given her $100.00 with which to decorate her room. She excitedly combs through magazines and catalogs to find the best prices on the items she wishes to buy.

Without using paper, pencil, or a calculator, does Jean have enough to buy . . .

1. the paint, border, blanket, bedspread, and pillows?_____

2. the ceiling fan, wall hanging, lamp, and chair? _____

3. the stuffed bear, bedspread, and paint?_____

List three possible combinations of items Jean may select with which to spend her $100.00.

4. _____

5. _____

6. _____

7. Roger likes to buy a milkshake at lunch three days each week. Milkshakes cost $1.25 each. About how much money does Roger spend each month? (**Hint:** There are about four weeks in each month.) _____

8. Farley dumps his piggy bank. He estimates that he has between 10 to 14 quarters, 25 to 29 dimes, 14 to 18 nickels, and 40 to 60 pennies. About how much money does Farley have? _____

To estimate numbers that have decimals, you might wish to round the decimal to the nearest whole number, similar to the way you round dollars and cents to the nearest whole dollar.

Example:

$$14.89 \longrightarrow 15 \qquad \$14.89 \longrightarrow \$15$$
$$\underline{+\ 12.99} \qquad \underline{+\ 13} \qquad \underline{+\ \$12.99} \qquad \underline{+\ \$13}$$
$$28 \qquad\qquad \$28$$

When multiplying and dividing, select rounded numbers to easily perform these operations.

Example:

$$179.83 \longrightarrow 200 \qquad \$179.83 \longrightarrow \$200.00$$
$$\underline{x\ 18.35} \longrightarrow \underline{x\ 20} \qquad \underline{x\ \$18.35} \longrightarrow \underline{x\ \$20.00}$$
$$4,000 \qquad\qquad \$4,000.00$$

Directions: Use the information above and on page 13 to solve these problems.

1. Evelyn and her mother are on their annual car trip. They travel 303.5 miles on the first day, 298.6 miles on the second day, and reach their destination after driving 261.7 miles on the third day. About how many miles did they travel to reach their destination? _____ About how many miles did they travel round trip? _____

2. Sue cuts 5 strings at random with which to make necklaces. They all measure between 42.6 and 58.8 cm. The beads each measure 1 cm. About how many beads will she use to complete her project? _____

These cities recorded the following rain amounts for the month of May. Use the data to answer the questions to the nearest whole inch.

City	Detroit	Milwaukee	Buffalo	Miami	Seattle
Rainfall (in inches)	2.9	2.8	3.1	6.2	1.8

3. How much more rain did Buffalo receive than Seattle? _____

4. About how much rain did Milwaukee and Detroit receive together? _____

5. If these cities can expect to receive similar rainfalls throughout the summer months (June, July, and August), approximately how much rain will they receive during the summer?

   Detroit _____   Buffalo _____   Seattle _____

   Milwaukee _____   Miami _____

6. Chris runs 3.4 miles each day. About how far will he run in one week? _____

Facts to Know

Many real-world problems deal with the concept of measurement. You may be asked to measure distance, capacity or volume, or weight or mass. Use the following conversions to answer measurement word problems.

Linear Measures

Use linear measurements to measure distance or the length, height, or width of an object. Depending on the length, you will need to decide whether to measure using large or small units of measurement. For example, you wouldn't want to measure the length of your driveway with inches, nor could you measure the length of the local pool with miles.

Customary Units of Length	Metric Units of Length
12 inches (in.) = 1 foot (ft.)	10 millimeters (mm) = 1 centimeter (cm)
3 feet (ft.) = 1 yard (yd.)	10 centimeters (cm) = 1 decimeter (dm)
5,280 feet (ft.) = 1 mile (mi.)	10 decimeters (dm) = 1 meter (m)
1,760 yards (yds.) = 1 mile (mi.)	100 centimeters (cm) = 1 meter (m)
	1,000 meters (m) = 1 kilometer (km)

Volume/Capacity

This is how much space a container takes up. For example, you may need to measure the capacity of an orange juice container to know how many fluid ounces of water to add to the mix to make orange juice.

Customary Units of Capacity	Metric Units of Capacity
2 tablespoons (Tbsp.) = 1 fluid ounce (fl. oz.)	100 milliliters (mL) = 1 deciliter (dL)
16 tablespoons (Tbsp.) = 1 cup (c.)	10 deciliters (dL) = 1 liter (L)
2 cups (c.) = 1 pint (pt.)	1,000 liters (L) = 1 kiloliter (kL)
2 pints (pt.) = 1 quart (qt.)	
4 quarts (qt.) = 1 gallon (gal.)	

Weight/Mass

Customary units measure an object's weight (how heavy it is). Metric measurements give an object's mass (how much matter it has). For example, you may need to follow the required weight and/or mass recommendations that allow you to carry a full backpack on a hike through the woods.

Customary Units of Weight	Metric Units of Mass
16 ounces (oz.) = 1 pound (lb.)	100 milligrams (mg) = 1 gram (g)
2,000 pounds (lbs.) = 1 ton	1,000 grams (g) = 1 kilogram (kg)

Directions: Use what you learned about linear measurements on page 17 to solve these word problems.

1. Bob runs errands with his older brother. They drive 2.6 miles to the post office, 1.8 miles to the store, and 0.6 miles to the bakery. From there they go 3.5 miles to the library. How far did the boys travel altogether? _____

2. A barnyard fence holds most of the animals on a small farm. The sides of the fence measure 348 feet, 78 feet, 211 feet, and 189 feet. How much longer is the longest side than the shortest? _____

3. Bill and his friends want to play ball. Rick helps Bill pace off the outfield. Would the boys most likely be measuring using inches, feet, or miles? _____

4. Robin is framing a picture, measuring 5 inches by 7 inches. She wishes to place a 2-inch mat around the outside of the picture. What will the perimeter of the frame measure? (**Hint:** To find the perimeter, measure the lengths of all the sides and add them together.) _____

5. Your parents are allowing you to decorate your room with a special wall border. The one you like comes in 5-yard units. You measure the walls and discover that the perimeter of your room is 46 feet. How many rolls of border will you need? _____

6. Rob wishes to run a 10-km (kilometer) race. To practice for the big event, he starts by running 1 km for two weeks, then adds 1.5 km to his run the third week and every three weeks thereafter. How long will it take for Rob to build up to 10 kilometers? _____

7. Jan biked the following number of kilometers each day. What is the average number of kilometers she biked for the week? (**Hint:** To find the average, add all of the totals and divide by the number of addends.)

_____

Day	Distance Biked
Monday	7 km
Tuesday	5 km
Wednesday	8 km
Thursday	9 km
Friday	6 km

8. Blaire discovered in science class that cumulonimbus clouds build to be 12,000 km high or higher. How many meters is this? _____

9. Milo cut a 6-meter piece of wood into four equal sections. How long was each piece, in centimeters? _____

10. Jill measures her birdhouse hole and finds that it has a 34-millimeter circumference. This is between which two centimeter measurements? _____

Directions: Use what you have learned on page 17 about volume and capacity to solve these word problems.

1. Jake mixes 1.5 L of white paint with 1.5 L of dark blue paint. How many liters of this lighter blue paint does he make? _____

2. Amy wishes to make 1.5 L of lemonade. The recipe calls for two parts water to one part lemon juice. How much water and juice will she add in milliliters?

_____

3. When Sal walks into science class, he sees three beakers, each filled with some liquid. The first has .5 L, the second 100 mL, and the third 125 mL. Which container has the largest amount? _____
How much more liquid is in the largest container than the smallest?_____

4. Vanessa's baby sister drinks between 175 mL to 225 mL of formula five times daily. How much liquid does the baby drink in a day? _____

5. Erin needs to take some liquid cough medicine. Should her dosage be measured in milliliters or liters?

_____

Why? _____

_____

_____

6. The Baker's pool has a capacity of 10,000 gallons. If they fill it at a rate of 400 gallons per hour, how many hours will it take to fill their pool to capacity?

_____

7. Eliza helps her mom make a fruit salad for a cookout. They add 1 cup each of watermelon, honeydew melon, bananas, and apples, 1/2 cup each of grapes, blueberries, and strawberries. How much salad did they make total?

_____

8. John brought an orange juice snack to his baseball team. He needed to bring enough to quench the thirst of his 15 teammates and himself. He estimated that each person needs about 2 cups. The orange juice comes in 16-ounce containers. How many pints does he need to bring to the team? _____

9. The class fish tank holds 10 gallons. If Emily uses a 2-cup container to fill the tank, how many times will she need to refill her container? _____

10. A drink mix calls for 1 scoop per 8 ounces of water. How many scoops would you need to fill a 2-quart container? (**Hint:** 8 ounces = 1 cup)

_____

Directions: Use what you learned on page 17 about weight and mass to solve these problems.

1. Mrs. Smith needs to know the weight of her car for insurance purposes. Will she inform her insurance agent of the ounces, pounds, or tons her car weighs? _____

2. All the heads of lettuce in the produce department weigh between 6 to 10 ounces. The lettuce is priced as marked. On average, what is the weight of the heads of lettuce? _____ Which type of lettuce is the best buy? _____

> Western $1.29 each
> Romaine   2 for $2.00
> Red Leaf $1.49 each

3. The maximum weight limit on a road is 10 tons. Butch's truck weighs 6 tons. He is carrying twenty-six 500-pound parcels. Will he make the weight limit? _____ By how much is he over or under the legal limit on this particular road? _____

4. The Smith's dog eats between 15 to 25 pounds of dog food each week. They buy Spot's food in 40-pound bags. How many bags do the Smiths buy to feed their dog each month? (**Hint:** one month = about 4 weeks) _____

5. Peter's dad wishes to invest in gold. He buys 6 ounces at $211 per ounce. How much money does he invest in all? _____ How much more gold would Peter's dad have to purchase to have a full pound? _____ Assuming the price of gold remains constant, how much more money would this be? _____

6. Georgina measures the fruit in her kitchen. She discovers that all the apples, grapes, and bananas have a total mass of 1,890 grams. How many kilograms is this?
_____

7. A crayon box lists the mass of each crayon as 4.7 grams. How many grams are in a box of 8 crayons? _____ 16 crayons? _____ 24 crayons? _____

	Food	Fat(g)
Breakfast	buttered toast	15 g
	juice	0 g
	milk	5 g
	coffee	0 g
	2 fried eggs	18 g
	2 bacon slices	25 g
Lunch	ham sandwich	10 g
	potato salad	12 g
	pickle	0 g
	soda	0 g
	apple	0 g

8. Milton is watching his fat intake. A man his size should be eating about 100 grams of fat per day. Look at the foods Milton has eaten so far today to determine how many more grams of fat he may eat at dinner. _____

9. Using Milton's food chart, determine how many more grams of fat he ate at breakfast than at lunch. _____

10. If Milton had been eating an average of 150 grams of fat per day, how many grams would this have been in one week? _____
On his new menu plan (100 g/day), how many grams of fat will he be taking in weekly? _____
How many fat grams per week is he saving?
_____

Facts to Know

Elapsed Time

These strategies will help you determine how much time has passed, whether it be minutes, hours, days, weeks, or months.

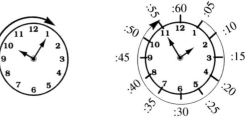

Hours   **Minutes**

1. Count the minutes and hours, forward or backward, on an actual clock. For example, to see how much time has passed between 10:05 A.M. and 1:55 P.M., count the minutes from :05 to :55 on the clock (:50), then the hours from 10 to 1 (3).

2. Another strategy is to add or subtract time as you would any other numbers. For P.M., add 12 hours to the hour. Regroup the minutes. Each hour has 60 minutes.

    Example:

       13 hours 55 minutes
     – 10 hours 05 minutes
        3 hours 50 minutes

       12 hours 45 minutes
     + 3 hours 25 minutes
      15 hours 70 minutes
    or 16 hours 10 minutes

June						
Sun	Mon	Tue	Wed	Thurs	Fri	Sat
				1	2	3
4	5	6	7	8	9	10
11	12	13	14	15	16	17
18	19	20	21	22	23	24
25	26	27	28	29	30	

3. Count the days and weeks on a calendar. Each week has 7 days. For example, a fishing trip is planned one summer. The group plans to leave at 8 A.M. on Sunday, June 18, and return at 5 P.M. on Friday, June 23. How long is the trip? Count the days, then the hours. From Sunday to Friday is 5 days. From 8:00 A.M. to 5:00 P.M. is 9 hours. The trip is planned to last 5 days, 9 hours.

Comparing and Measuring Time

Use the elapsed time strategies to compare and measure time. For example, if two teams have a race to see who can make it more quickly from their campsite to the lake, first measure how long each team took to race, then compare the two times by subtracting the totals.

Example: Team A's time is 2 minutes 8 seconds.
Team B's time is 1 minute 44 seconds.
How much longer did Team A take than Team B?
Regroup 1 minute to 60 seconds.

   2 min. 08 sec.
– 1 min. 44 sec.
  0 min. 24 sec.

Use this table to convert time.

Time Conversions	
60 seconds (sec.) = 1 minute (min.)	365 days = 1 year (yr.)
60 minutes (min.) = 1 hour (hr.)	366 days = 1 leap year
24 hours (hr.) = 1 day	10 years = 1 decade
7 days = 1 week	10 decades = 1 century
28–31 days = 1 month (mo.)	10 centuries = 1 millennium

Directions: Use what you learned on page 21 about determining how much time has elapsed to solve the following problems.

Use the bus schedule to answer questions 1–4.

Bus Schedule

Destination	Departure Time
Dallas, TX	7:08 A.M.
Butte, MT	9:18 A.M.
Denver, CO	11:51 A.M.
Nashville, TN	1:36 P.M.
Oakland, CA	3:40 P.M.

1. How much time elapses between the first bus departure and the last? _____

2. Glenda arrives at the bus station at 1:15 P.M. to catch the Nashville bus. How long is her wait at the bus depot? _____

3. The Oakland bus is due to arrive in Oakland at 3:15 A.M. the following day. How long is the bus ride?

   _____

4. Jenna wishes to give herself at least 15 minutes at the bus depot before leaving for Denver, Colorado. She estimates her car ride from home to the depot to be about 38 minutes. What is the latest Jenna should leave her house? _____

5. Bonnie arrived home at 4:34 P.M. After school, she spent 13 minutes talking to her friends, 23 minutes at the library, and 28 minutes on the bus. At what time is Bonnie's school dismissed? _____

6. Students file into the cafeteria by class every three minutes. There are 30 classes that have a planned lunchtime. The first lunch begins at 11:10 A.M. When is the last lunch scheduled? _____

Use the monthly calendars to answer questions 7–10.

September						
Sun	Mon	Tue	Wed	Thurs	Fri	Sat
						1
2	3	4	5	6	7	8
9	10	11	12	13	14	15
16	17	18	19	20	21	22
30 23	24	25	26	27	28	29

October						
Sun	Mon	Tue	Wed	Thurs	Fri	Sat
	1	2	3	4	5	6
7	8	9	10	11	12	13
14	15	16	17	18	19	20
21	22	23	24	25	26	27
28	29	30	31			

November						
Sun	Mon	Tue	Wed	Thurs	Fri	Sat
				1	2	3
4	5	6	7	8	9	10
11	12	13	14	15	16	17
18	19	20	21	22	23	24
25	26	27	28	29	30	

December						
Sun	Mon	Tue	Wed	Thurs	Fri	Sat
						1
2	3	4	5	6	7	8
9	10	11	12	13	14	15
16	17	18	19	20	21	22
30 23	31 24	25	26	27	28	29

7. A new movie is opening up on October 20. It is due to close on December 1 unless sales are still way up at this time. How long is the movie supposed to stay open?

   _____

8. The film coordinators from problem 7 need to plan their advertising strategies. They usually begin advertising three weeks prior to the movie opening date. They need at least 10 days to plan their advertising strategies and marketing techniques. What is the latest date that they should start this planning? _____

9. Marla's father has a 6-day business trip scheduled in November. He is due to leave on the 14th. When will he return? _____

10. The last day of the grading period for one school semester is Friday, December 21. If the grading period is 45 school days long, on what day did it start? (**Remember:** There is no school on Thursday and Friday, November 22 and 23, for the Thanksgiving holiday.)

_____

5 ▶ Practice •••••••••••• Solving Word Problems That Compare and Measure Time

Directions: Use what you learned on page 21 about comparing and measuring time to answer the following questions.

Test Schedule

Day 1	Day 2
70 min. test	60 min. test
10 min. test	10 min. test
40 min. test	45 min. test

1. The fifth graders are preparing to take required tests. If the testing goes as scheduled and the students need an additional 5 minutes before and 5 minutes after each test to distribute and collect materials, what is the total test time for the two days? _____

2. Melanie counts the commercial minutes for each 30-minute television segment starting at 7:00 P.M. and ending at 9 P.M. The table shows her findings. If this collection of data is fairly representative of weekday primetime shows, then how many commercial minutes might a viewer expect to see during these times on Monday through Friday?

_____

Commercial Minutes
(7:00 P.M.–9:00 P.M.)

Show time	Commercial Minutes
7:00 P.M.	9 min. 19 sec.
7:30 P.M.	10 min. 14 sec.
8:00 P.M.	9 min. 49 sec.
8:30 P.M.	8 min. 38 sec.

3. Melissa wishes to make dinner for her family one evening. She reads the package directions and sees that she can expect to spend 15 minutes preparing the meal, 50 minutes baking it, and an additional 5 minutes allowing it to set before serving. How much time does Melissa need before dinner is served? _____

   If she wishes to have dinner ready by 6:00 P.M., what is the latest time she should start cooking? _____

4. Jackie wants to make the most cookies possible in the shortest amount of time. The package directions for Jammin' Jimmie's Cookies state that the cookies take 6 minutes to bake and that the yield is 5 dozen cookies. The directions for the Sensational Sugar Cookies package state that the cookies take 8 minutes to bake and the yield is 4 dozen cookies. Jackie determines that she can fit 20 rounded teaspoons of the first cookie on each tray and 24 rounded teaspoons of the second cookie on each tray, following the package directions for spacing. Which cookie yields more cookies per minute? **(Hint:** one dozen = 12 cookies) _____

5. Gil spends 6 hours and 23 minutes painting a scene for the school play. The play lasts 1 hour and 12 minutes. How much longer did Gil spend painting the scenery than the play lasted? _____

6. A sales clerk at a clothing store is interested in charting her sales for the day. At 1:00 P.M., her sales total $358. At 3:00 P.M., she has $716, and at 5:00 P.M., her sales total $1,432. If this trend continues, how much in sales can she expect to have at 7:00 P.M.? _____ How much will the final sales total at the 9:00 P.M. closing time? _____

5 Practice • • • • • • • • • • Solving Word Problems That Require Time Conversions

Directions: Use the chart on page 21 to help you discover the answers to these problems. You may need to convert time from hours to minutes, months to years, etc.

1. Katrina wishes to walk dogs for a summer job. Her summer lasts about 13 weeks. After advertising her services, she receives 18 jobs, earning $15 per client per week. She spends about 1 hour 30 minutes daily with each group of dogs, walking 5 at a time for five days each week. How much of her summer vacation in days will Katrina be spending "on the job"? _____

2. Hal and his friends wait in line for 68 minutes for a particular ride they like at an amusement park. The ride lasts only 2 minutes and 16 seconds. How many seconds is their wait for every 1 second of the ride? _____

3. An airplane pilot spends roughly 4 to 6 hours a day in the air. If he works 50 weeks out of the year (a workweek is 5 days long), about how many months will he spend flying? _____

4. Presidential elections occur once every four years. How many times will the public vote for a new president in one century? _____

5. A pizza runs through a pizza oven about every 3 minutes 45 seconds. The restaurant manager claims he cooks roughly 40 pizzas in one night. How much time in hours does he spend baking pizzas? _____

6. Mrs. Rogers has three children. The oldest is 7 years old. The youngest is 70 months younger than the oldest. How old is her youngest child? _____ Her second child is about 1,500 days older than the youngest. How old is the second child? _____

7. An upcoming space mission is scheduled to occur in three phases. The first phase lasts about 8 months, the second phase about 18 months, and the final phase about 13 months. How many years is this space project? _____

8. Henry's CD songs total 1,410 minutes. How many hours of songs does he own? _____

9. A leap year occurs every four years. How many leap years are there between the years 1900 and 2200, inclusive? _____

10. Kirk calculates that his basketball takes 18 seconds to bounce ten times. His rubber ball takes 26 seconds to bounce ten times. How many times would he have to continuously bounce his basketball and rubber ball for them to finish their 10 bounces at the same time? _____ How many minutes will have passed? _____

Facts to Know

Adding or Subtracting Fractions

To add or subtract fractions, be sure that all the fractions have like denominators. *Add or subtract the numerators while keeping the denominators the same.*

$$\frac{4}{5} - \frac{3}{5} = \frac{1}{5} \qquad\qquad \frac{3}{7} + \frac{2}{7} = \frac{5}{7}$$

If the fractions have unlike denominators, *determine the least common denominator and convert the fractions.*

$$\frac{3}{5} + \frac{3}{10} = \qquad\qquad \frac{3}{5} \times \frac{2}{2} = \frac{6}{10} \qquad\qquad \frac{6}{10} + \frac{3}{10} = \frac{9}{10}$$

Multiplying Fractions

To multiply fractions, *multiply the numerators and the denominators.*

$$\frac{1}{4} \times \frac{3}{5} = \frac{3}{20}$$

Dividing Fractions

To divide fractions, *multiply the dividend by the reciprocal of the divisor.*

$$\frac{2}{3} \div \frac{1}{4} = \frac{2}{3} \times \frac{4}{1} = \frac{8}{3} \text{ or } 2\frac{2}{3}$$

Computing with Whole Numbers

When adding, subtracting, multiplying, or dividing whole numbers, *rewrite the whole number as a fraction.*

$$3 \times \frac{1}{5} = \frac{3}{1} \times \frac{1}{5} = \frac{3}{5} \qquad\qquad 2 - \frac{1}{3} = \frac{6}{3} - \frac{1}{3} = \frac{5}{3} \text{ or } 1\frac{2}{3}$$

Computing with Mixed Numbers

When adding, subtracting, multiplying, or dividing mixed numbers, *write the numbers as improper fractions (where the numerator is larger than the denominator). Multiply the whole number by the denominator, then add the numerator.* This number becomes your new numerator.

$$4\frac{4}{5} = \quad 4 \times 5 = 20; \quad 20 + 4 = 24 \qquad\qquad 4\frac{4}{5} = \frac{24}{5}$$

To change a fraction to a mixed number, *divide the numerator by the denominator.* This becomes the whole number and the remainder becomes the fractional number. Use the same denominator.

$$\frac{24}{5} = 24 \div 5 = 4R4 = 4\frac{4}{5}$$

Lowest Terms

To write a fraction in lowest terms, be sure neither the numerator nor the denominator have any common factors. *Divide the numerator and denominator by the greatest common factor.*

$$\frac{6}{10} = \frac{6}{10} \div \frac{2}{2} = \frac{3}{5}$$

Directions: Use the information on page 25 to solve these word problems that require the addition, subtraction, multiplication, or division of fractional parts. Write each fraction in lowest terms.

1. Helen determines that 2/11 of one package of colored candies is red. When she opens a second package, she determines that 7/11 are red. How many more red candies make up the second package than the first? _____

2. Two teams of eight people wish to play a game of dodge ball. When combining the two teams, five members of the first team are ruled out within five minutes (5/16). Only three members of the second team are ruled out within five minutes (3/16). What fractional portion of the teams were ruled out within the first five minutes in all? _____

3. Marsha's mom went on some errands. Once she was in town, she drove 1/4 mile to get to the post office, 3/10 mile to the bakery, and 1/2 mile to the dry cleaners. How far did Marsha's mom drive around town? _____

4. In his garage, John found 2/3 of a piece of plywood he could use to make a birdhouse. He ended up only using 5/6 of the remaining 2/3 board. How much of the original board did he need? _____

5. When selling candy as a field trip fund-raiser, the students decided to pool the leftover candy and sell it at a local grocery store. Jan had 2/3 of a box left, Mike 1/4 of a box, and George had 5/6 of his box left to sell. How many boxes of candy do the students have left to sell in all?_____

6. Sarah used 2/3 of a bag of flour that was half full to make a cake. How much flour did Sarah need for her cake? _____

7. Dan finds a cookie recipe, but it yields six dozen cookies. He figures he can make 1/3 of the recipe to make just the two dozen cookies he needs. The recipe calls for 2 cups of flour and 1 cup sugar. How much flour and sugar will Dan need to make 1/3 of the recipe? _____

8. When Mrs. Harold's class did a pet survey, they found that the total number of cats owned by her students was 9. This is 3/4 as many as the number of dogs. How many dogs do the students own? _____

9. In health class the students discovered that the average weight of the girls in their class was 88 lbs. This figure is 4/5 the average weight of the boys. What is the average weight of the boys in health class? _____

10. Two-thirds of a typical delivery truck includes 110 parcels. How many parcels typically make up a whole truck? _____

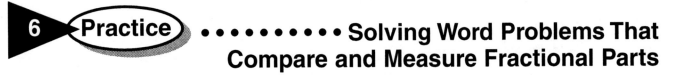

6 ▶Practice • • • • • • • • • • **Solving Word Problems That Compare and Measure Fractional Parts**

Before comparing fractions, be sure all of the denominators are the same.

Directions: Use the information on page 25 to solve the following word problems that require the measurement and/or comparison of fractional parts.

1. Flora is helping her younger sister make paper bag puppets. For the dog they needed 1/2 sheet of black paper, for the cat they used 2/3 sheet of black paper, and for the pig they needed 1/6 sheet of black paper. Which paper bag puppet required the most black paper? _____

2. Of the 27 students in Mr. Drake's math class, 18 have brown eyes. What fraction of Mr. Drake's math students have brown eyes? _____

3. Libby spent 1/4 of her $10.00 on new pencils, 2/5 of her $10.00 on hair clips, and 3/10 of her $10.00 on candy. On which item did she spend the most money? _____

4. Using the information from problem number 3, find out how much money Libby had left over from her $10.00. _____

5. Eight hundred and forty people responded to a recent Internet survey. Part of the survey asked the participants to identify their age status. Two hundred and eighty fell in the 18 to 30 age range, 350 fell in the 31 to 50 age range, and 210 were over 50. What fractional number of people responded for each age range? _____

6. During the second election, Casper received 1/3 of the student vote, Carl received 1/5 of the student vote, and Flora received 7/15 of the student vote. Who won the election?

_____

7. Determining which method of advertisement is most effective, the students took a survey in their class. One half thought packaging was most effective, 1/3 thought taste or flavor was most effective, and 1/6 thought catchy phrases sold more products. Which kind of advertising did most students think was the most effective? _____

8. In problem 7 above, 12 people agreed that taste or flavor was the most effective advertising tools. How many people thought packaging and catchy phrases were more effective advertising strategies? _____

9. When trying out their paper airplane models, Jake's team flew 2/3 the distance of the hallway, Ryan's team flew 7/12 the distance of the hallway, and Ginger's team flew 3/4 the distance of the hallway. Which team's airplane flew the farthest? _____

10. Florence has selected a 434-page book to read for her next novel assignment. She can only keep the book for two weeks. What fractional portion of the book must she read daily to finish the book in the required time? _____ How many pages is this per day? _____

Time: Every minute is 1/60 of an hour. Every 5 minutes = 1/12 of an hour.

Linear Measures: Inches are divided into 1/16 units on a ruler. Four 1/16 units = 1/4 inch.
Metric units are base 10. 1/10 cm = 1 millimeter; 1/100 meter = 1 cm, etc.

Capacity: Customary units are just fractional portions of one another. 1/4 gal. = 1 qt.;
1/2 pint = 1 cup; 1/2 cup = 4 ounces, etc.

Directions: Use the information on pages 17 and 21 to solve these fraction word problems involving time or measurement. Write your answers in lowest terms.

1. Tyler has brought 3 gallons of punch to school for a class party. He has figured this to be enough for everyone to have two 1-cup servings. How many people does he plan to serve? _____

2. Gail bought 2½ pounds of ground coffee at the store. She'll use about 1/10 this amount each day to make a pot of coffee. How much ground coffee does she use each morning? _____

3. The Giles' driveway is 1/2 mile long. Their construction company has sectioned it off into fourths. How long, in feet, is each section? _____

4. Blaire practiced his trumpet 1³⁄₁₀ hours on Monday and Thursday, 4/5 hour on Tuesday, and 1½ hours Wednesday and Friday. He is supposed to practice 5 hours each week. Did he succeed? _____ How many hours did Blaire practice? _____

5. Gina's race time was 1/4 minute shorter than Glenda's. By how many seconds did Gina win? _____

6. Kelly wishes to make a Halloween costume out of the fabric pieces her mother has left over from other projects. She finds 1¾ yards of blue with white polka dots, 2½ yards of green with yellow stripes, and 1⅞ yards of black with red hearts. How many linear yards of fabric does Kelly have to work with? _____ How much is this in inches?
_____

7. Brian has to order the letters of a particular font from thinnest to widest. He discovers that 10 letters are 1/5 cm wide, 6 letters are 1/10 cm wide, 6 letters are 3/10 cm wide, and 4 are 2/5 cm wide. What fraction of the letters are 1/5 cm wide? _____

8. Students' model drawings of national monuments measure 8½ inches, 6¾ inches, 5⅞ inches, and 3¾ inches. List these heights from shortest to tallest.

_____

7 ▶ How to • • • • • • • • • • • • • • • • • Solve Word Problems Involving Geometry

Facts to Know

Geometric Shapes

Polygons are two-dimensional figures made up of several line segments. All polygons have straight sides and 3 or more angles. Remember these polygons' names and characteristics when solving word problems involving geometric shapes.

- A *triangle* has three sides and three angles with the sum of the inside angles measuring 180°.
- An *equilateral* triangle has three sides that are equal in length with each angle measuring 60°.
- An *isosceles* triangle has two sides that are equal in length.
- A *scalene* triangle has no equal sides or angles.
- An *obtuse* triangle has one angle that measures greater than 90°.
- A *right* triangle has one angle that measures exactly 90°.
- A *quadrilateral* has four sides and four angles with the sum of the inside angles measuring 360°.
- A *square* has all four sides equal in length with all four angles measuring 90°.
- A *rectangle* has two pairs of opposite sides equal in length with all the angles measuring 90°.
- A *pentagon* has five sides and five angles.
- A *hexagon* has six sides and six angles.
- An *octagon* has eight sides and eight angles.
- A *decagon* has 10 sides and 10 angles.

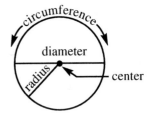

Circles are not polygons because they are not made up of angles and line segments. A circle measures 360° around its center. A circle has the same radius measure to any outward point from its center. A circle's diameter is the distance through the center of the circle. A circle's circumference is the distance around the outside of the circle.

Perimeter of Polygons

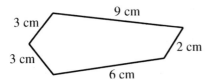

To find a shape's perimeter, add the lengths of all the sides of the figure.

3 cm + 3 cm + 6 cm + 2 cm + 9 cm = 3 cm

Area of Polygons

- To find the area of closed plane figures, count the square units that make up the figure's surface.
- To find the area of a rectangle or square, multiply the length by the width to find the square units that make up the figure's area.

Volume of Rectangular Prisms

A rectangular prism is a three-dimensional shape that has rectangular faces on all six sides. Some of the faces may be squares. A rectangular prism that has all square faces is called a *cube*. To find the volume, or how much space the inside of the rectangular prism has, multiply the length by the width by the height. Write the volume in cubic measurements. The formula looks like this:

volume = length (l) x width (w) x height (h)

Directions: Use what you learned on page 29 to solve the following word problems that require you to illustrate your findings.

1. Gerry and his friends walk a baseball diamond in a large field. When they finish, home plate to first base measures 50 feet, first to second measures 40 feet, second to third measures 50 feet, and third to home measures 60 feet. Draw what the field may have looked like. Did the boys pace a perfectly-square field?

———————————

2. Helen is very proud of the patchwork doll she received from her grandmother. She has counted 32 small squares, 16 small triangles, 14 small circles, and 26 small rectangles that make up the doll's exterior. Draw a picture of Helen's doll. How many polygons make up the doll?

———————————

3. Vera and her two friends created a tent with an old blanket and clothesline. The top angle of the tent measures about 100°. When the two sides are secured to the ground, one measures 37 inches, the other 40 inches. Draw what the tent looked like in the space provided. What kind of triangle did the girls create?

———————————

4. Jeremiah is building a storage case for his bedroom. The case measures 18 inches deep by 30 inches wide by 36 inches high. He wishes to include three shelf spaces by securing two boards. One shelf he wishes to be 10 inches high and a second 12 inches high. Draw what the shelves will look like. How tall will the third shelf space be? What is the volume of each shelf space?

———————————

Directions: Use what you learned on page 29 to solve the following word problems that require you to compute the area, volume, or perimeter.

1. Jason and his friends built a fort in his room with his bedsheets and clothespins. Once it was all finished, the outside face had a pentagonal shape. The outside face of the fort had a perimeter of 140 inches. Two sides measured 40 inches and 35 inches. What was the total length of the other three sides of the pentagonal shape?

   _____

2. The Fenners are building a square pool. The pool will have a perimeter of 90 feet. They wish to have it built to yield the greatest surface area possible. What will each of the four sides measure, in feet, to give them the greatest possible surface area? _____

3. Meghan's blanket has a surface area of 40 square feet. List the possible lengths and widths of the blanket, then circle the one that most likely shows the dimensions of the blanket.

   _____

4. Craig has some new spiral drawing tools. The diameters of the circular pieces measure 3 inches, 5 inches, and 7 inches. What is the radius of each of the circular pieces? _____

5. A picnic basket measures 20 inches long by 12 inches wide by 12 inches high. What is the volume of the picnic basket? _____

6. Jake and his family are going on a picnic. The box of fried chicken has a volume of 432 cubic inches, the container of salad has a volume of 175 cubic inches, and the container of fruit has a volume of 112 cubic inches. The plates, utensils, and cups make up 500 cubic inches. Can they fit all of these items into their basket if they use the basket with the dimensions from problem 5 above? _____

   _____

7. The Henderson boys built their dog an unusually shaped doghouse. The floor had eight sides as it appears in the diagram below. Use the grid key to determine the surface area of the floor of the doghouse.

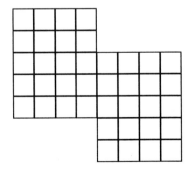

Key ☐ = 1 sq. ft.

Directions: Use the map of My Town, U.S.A. on page 33, a protractor, a centimeter ruler, and the information below to answer the following questions.

To measure angles with a protractor, place the hole of the protractor over the vertex (or point) of the angle. Begin measuring from 0°. Measure the degrees where the second ray intersects the protractor.

1. Another tour group has just toured the Mayor's House. They leave by way of the north side of the building, then head east to the second intersection. There they make a 90° right turn. At the next intersection, they make a 90° right turn. They follow this to the next intersection and make a left turn. How many degrees is the turn? _____

2. Jenny wished to visit a sick friend in the hospital. At which bus stop would she most likely depart the bus? _____ About how far from the nearest bus stop is the hospital? _____

3. Howie is at bus stop C. He walks to the Art Museum by following the route around Town Circle. How many degrees around the circle does he walk? _____

4. Gina and her friends are at bus stop A. They go south to the first street on their right and head to Town Circle, then take the road that is at a 150° angle from the road they were on. Which building are they likely to visit? _____

5. A school group just left the Art Museum. About how far a walk west do they have before they reach Town Hall? _____

6. What would you estimate the area of City Park to be in square miles? _____

Example

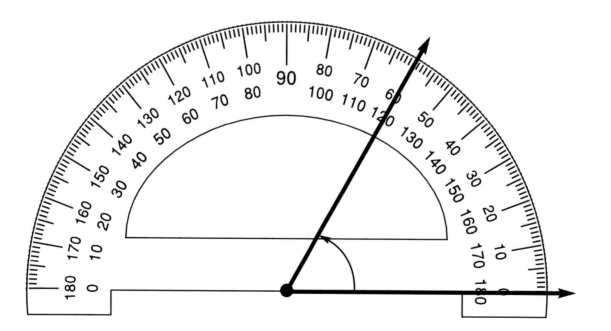

My Town, U.S.A.

This map shows the locations of some tourist sites and other general buildings in My Town, U.S.A.

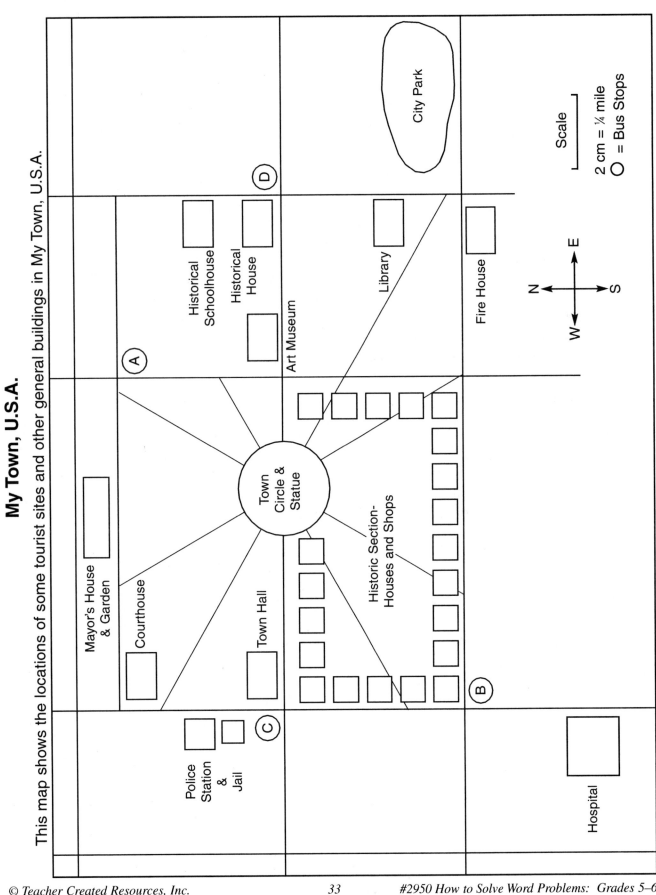

Scale

2 cm = ¼ mile
O = Bus Stops

Facts to Know

Some word problems may require you to conduct two or more steps before coming to the final answer.
Consider this problem.

> Marcus has 45 minutes to finish as much homework as he can before dinner. When reviewing his
> planner, he estimates he has 20 minutes of reading, 20 minutes of math, 15 minutes of writing,
> and a science fair project planning sheet that will probably take 10 minutes. If Marcus maximizes
> his time before dinner, how much more homework will he have to complete after dinner?

Follow the Four-Step Plan (See page 5)

Step 1: Read and Understand the Problem

— Why is this problem important? *Marcus can maximize his time.*

— What do I need to find out? *I need to find out how much homework Marcus has after dinner.*

— What information do I know? *I know how much homework he has in each subject and the
amount of time he has before dinner.*

— Do I have all of the information I need to solve it? *Yes, I do.*

Step 2: Make a Plan

1. Add up all of the minutes of homework Marcus has.

2. Subtract 45 minutes from this total.

3. Find out how much more homework Marcus has beyond 45 minutes.

Step 3: Solve the Problem

$$
\begin{aligned}
20 &\text{ minutes reading} \\
20 &\text{ minutes math} \\
15 &\text{ minutes writing} \\
+\ 10 &\text{ minutes science} \\
\hline
65 &\text{ minutes of homework} \\
-\ 45 &\text{ minutes before dinner} \\
\hline
20 &\text{ minutes homework after dinner}
\end{aligned}
$$

Step 4: Check to Be Sure Your Answer Makes Sense

When you read the original problem, did you expect Marcus to have an abundance of homework after
dinner? Probably not. You can estimate his total homework time to be about an hour. This is just a
little over the 45 minutes he has before dinner. Our answer of 20 minutes makes sense.

8 ▷ Practice • • • • • Solving Multi-Step Word Problems

Directions: Use what you learned on pages 5 and 34 to solve these multi-step word problems. Be sure to pay careful attention to whether you should add, subtract, multiply, divide, or perform two or more of these operations to solve the problems.

1. Erin needs to buy 2 sheets of plywood, 6 dowels, and 3 two-by-fours for a building project. The plywood costs $2.65 per sheet, the dowels $0.39 each, and the two-by-fours $0.89 each. How much is her subtotal, without tax? _____

2. Claire and two of her fifth grade friends went to the movies Saturday afternoon. Each girl bought one ticket, one popcorn, and one large soda. How much money did the three girls spend altogether? _____

Movie and Snack Bar Prices			
adult ticket	$7.00	small soda	$1.75
under 17	$5.00	large soda	$2.25
under 3	$3.00	small candy	$2.25
popcorn	$2.50	large candy	$3.25

3. Bob bought a new bike. The bike cost $129.95 with tax. He gave the cashier $150.00. The bike also comes with a $10.00 mail-in rebate. How much will Bob get back, including the rebate? _____

4. Yvonne travels 4.8 miles to get to town. Once there, she drives 3.7 miles to run her errands. After she returns home, she realizes she forgot to go to the pet shop for some special fish food. This trip to town is 6.2 miles. Once she finally reaches home after all her errands, the odometer on the car reads 36,835.3 miles. What did the odometer read before she started for town the first time? _____

5. Mrs. Carlson wants to be sure all of the students have equal access to the Halloween candy she brought to share throughout the day. She has two packages each of Peanut Butter Buddies, Chocolate Chewies, and Caramel Creamies. The Peanut Butter Buddies have an estimated 24 pieces per bag, the Chocolate Chewies about 36 per bag, and the Caramel Creamies about 30 pieces per bag. Mrs. Carlson plans to place one bowl of mixed candy at each of 7 sets of tables in her classroom. About how many pieces of candy will each bowl have? _____

6. In an elementary school, the kindergarten through third grade classes, of which there are four in each grade level, receive 30 minutes daily of instruction time for special classes such as art, music, drama, gym, etc. The fourth and fifth grade classes, of which there are five in each grade level, receive 40 minutes daily for special classes. How many total hours of the school day do all the classes spend in special classes? _____

8 ⊳ Practice ••••• Solving Multi-Step Word Problems Involving Money

Directions: Use what you learned on page 34 and the prices below to solve these multi-step word problems involving money. You will need to know how to compute totals with tax. Follow the steps below.

To compute totals with tax . . .

1. Subtotal the cost of the item(s).
2. Multiply the subtotal by the tax rate.
3. Add the tax to the subtotal.

Alexa's Electronics

Electronic Items	In-store prices	Online prices
personal cassette player	$39.99	$36.79
personal CD player	$179.99	$165.59
mini disc player	$229.99	$211.59
stereo receiver	$129.99	$119.59
stereo CD player	$149.99	$137.99
stereo cassette player	$119.99	$110.39
stereo speakers (1 pair)	$89.99	$82.79
CD boom box	$59.99	$55.19
CD boom box with cassette	$79.99	$73.59
larger CD/cassette boom box	$169.99	$156.39
electric drum set	$109.99	$101.19
headphones	$19.99	$18.39

1. Sue buys a new personal cassette player at the store. She pays 6% sales tax. What is the total cost of her purchase? _____

2. Paul orders a pair of speakers and headphones online. He pays no sales tax, but shipping costs an additional 15% of his purchase price. How much does Paul's order come to? _____

3. Lisa knows the stereo receiver she wants is going on sale for 10% off the in-store price this weekend. Is this more or less than the online price? _____

4. Devon orders a new CD boom box with cassette online. He pays no tax, but shipping costs an additional 15% of his purchase price. Would he have saved money had he gone to the store and paid the in-store price with 6% tax? _____

5. Gerald buys the electric drum set with headphones at Alexa's Electronics. He pays 6% sales tax. He pays with one $50 bill and five $20 bills. How much change does Gerald receive? _____

• • • • • Solving Multi-Step Word Problems Involving Measurement

Directions: Use what you learned on page 34 and the conversion tables from page 17 to solve these multi-step word problems involving measurement.

Fiona is making a cake for a school fund-raiser. The list of ingredients appears on the left. When Fiona looks through her cabinets, she finds that she has the ingredients and quantities listed on the right. Help Fiona determine whether she has enough of each item to make 1, 2, or 3 cakes. If not, determine how much more she needs to buy.

Ingredients	Needed	Available
flour	1½ cups	64 oz.
sugar	¾ cup	10 oz.
baking soda	1 tbsp.	1 oz.
baking powder	½ tbsp.	6 oz.
cocoa	½ cup	10 oz.
eggs	3	½ dozen
vanilla	½ tbsp	none
cherries	1 cup	2 oz.

Check whether Fiona has enough of each item to make the following number of cakes. If she does not have enough, write the quantity, in ounces, showing how much more she needs.

	enough for 1 cake?	quantity needed	enough for 2 cakes?	quantity needed	enough for 3 cakes?	quantity needed
1. flour	_____	_____	_____	_____	_____	_____
2. sugar	_____	_____	_____	_____	_____	_____
3. baking soda	_____	_____	_____	_____	_____	_____
4. baking powder	_____	_____	_____	_____	_____	_____
5. cocoa	_____	_____	_____	_____	_____	_____
6. eggs	_____	_____	_____	_____	_____	_____
7. vanilla	_____	_____	_____	_____	_____	_____
8. cherries	_____	_____	_____	_____	_____	_____

9 ▶ How to ·······Solve Algebraic Word Problems

Facts to Know

Exponents

Sometimes you might need to find large quantities of numbers quickly. An *exponential notation* expresses the repeated multiplication of a number. The following example shows "3 to the 4th power."

$$3^4 \qquad = 3 \times 3 \times 3 \times 3 \qquad = 81$$
(exponential notation) \qquad (expanded form) \qquad (standard form)

A number "raised to the second power" is said to be squared. A number "raised to the third power" is said to be cubed.

$$5^2 \text{ (5 squared)} = 5 \times 5 = 25 \qquad\qquad 6^3 \text{ (6 cubed)} = 6 \times 6 \times 6 = 216$$

Algebraic Equations

Sometimes when a quantity is unknown, mathematicians use letters to represent the unknown quantities. Note the following examples:

Addition	$w + 3 = 5$	Multiplication	$3y = 21$
Subtraction	$3 - x = 0$	Division	$8/z = 2$

In the above examples, the letters are unknown quantities, or variables. You may solve the equations to assign quantities to the variables. These solutions make the above equations true.

$$w = 2 \qquad\qquad x = 3 \qquad\qquad y = 7 \qquad\qquad z = 4$$

Finding Algebraic Equations Through Patterns

Using the "find a pattern" problem-solving method may lead to an algebraic equation. Consider the following situation.

> Barney is building a geometric tower with gumdrops and straws. He starts with 1 straw and 2 gumdrops, then he adds 1 straw and 1 gumdrop with each addition to his tower. How many straws and gumdrops does Barney need to complete his twentieth addition? his hundredth?

Use the chart to find a pattern. Use the letter s (for straws) and g (for gumdrops) in an algebraic equation to find the answers to the questions.

$$s = g - 1 \qquad \text{or} \qquad g = s + 1$$

Insert the given number of straws (s) to find the number of gumdrops (g) to be used.

Solve for g.

s	g
1	2
2	3
3	4
4	5
5	6
20	—
100	—

$$g_1 = s + 1 \qquad\qquad g_2 = s + 1$$
$$g_1 = 20 + 1 \qquad\qquad g_2 = 100 + 1$$
$$g_1 = 21 \qquad\qquad g_2 = 101$$

Directions: Use what you learned about squared numbers, cubed numbers, and exponents on page 38 to solve the following problems.

1. Sue, who worked at a pet shop, was responsible for stocking the dog food shelves. She counted six rows and six columns of food, each in six sections of the aisle. Sue remembered that since this involved repeated multiplication, she could cube the base. Write the exponential notation she used to find out how many different kinds of dog food the store sold. _____

2. Jerome, chairman of the board for a large computer company, is looking to merge with a smaller company. He estimates their combined assets to total an estimated $3.8 x 10^7. How much is this? _____

Find out how many miles each of these planets is from the sun.

3. Mercury   36 x 10^6 _____

4. Venus   67 x 10^6 _____

5. Saturn   9 x 10^8 _____

6. Neptune   2.8 x 10^9 _____

Helga measures her room for new carpet. It is 144 feet^2. The length of her room is the same as its width.

7. How long is Helga's room?_____

8. How wide is it? _____

9. If Helga had 12-foot ceilings in her room, what would the volume of her room be? (**Hint:** *volume = length* x *width* x *height*) _____

10. Kerri estimates she cut between 2^7 and 2^8 pieces of confetti for a surprise party. How many pieces of confetti did Kerri make? _____

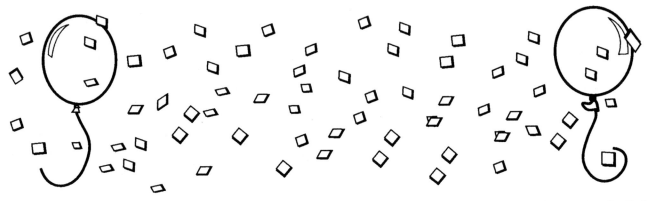

Directions: Use what you learned on page 38 to write an algebraic equation for each situation.

Situation	Algebraic Equation
1. A roll of candy had 10 pieces. Hugh ate *p* pieces. Four pieces remained.	_____
2. Bob and John together are 105 inches tall. John is 53 inches tall. Bob is *b* inches tall.	_____
3. Three pictures in a pattern are repeated *y* times. There are 96 pictures total.	_____
4. Kerra shared 100 pieces of popcorn equally among *t* people. Each person received 25 pieces.	_____
5. A building has 108 offices. Each of *w* stories has 12 offices.	_____

Directions: Use what you learned on page 38 to write an equation for each situation. Then solve for the unknown quantity.

Situation	Algebraic Equation	Solution
6. The Empire State Building in New York City, built in 1931, is 1,250 feet tall. One World Trade Center, completed in 1972, is *d* feet taller, measuring 1,368 feet in height. How much higher is One World Trade Center than the Empire State Building?	_____	_____
7. Kiki's class sold school pens for a fund-raiser. Each box held *g* pens. They sold 12 boxes for a total of 1,728 pens. How many pens are in each box?	_____	_____
8. At the end of the day, Mrs. Marcus gives some students a reward of 2 pieces of red-hot candy balls. On Monday, she gave out a total of 18 candies. How many students (*s*) received the reward on Monday?	_____	_____

Directions: Use what you learned on page 38 to continue the T-chart patterns. Then solve for the unknown quantity.

> Beatrice builds cubes with large marshmallows (*m*) and straws (*s*). For each cube she needs 8 marshmallows and 12 straws. The chart shows her progress as she continues to build cubes. Fill in the chart for the next three builds.

1. How much do the *m* values increase with each cube? _____

2. How much do the *s* values increase with each cube? _____

3. How many marshmallows does Beatrice use with the unknown *s* quantity?
_____

4. Use the algebraic equation to solve for *s*. _____

m	s
8	12
16	24
24	36
—	—
—	—
—	—
80	s

$$s = 3 \times \tfrac{1}{2}\,m$$

> Rafael builds a geometric dome using clay (*c*) and toothpicks (*t*). He starts with 4 clay balls and 6 toothpicks. He adds 2 clay balls and 3 toothpicks each time as he makes it bigger. The chart shows his progress and the pattern. Continue the pattern for the next three additions.

5. How much do the *c* values increase each time? _____

6. How much do the *t* values increase each time? _____

7. How many clay balls does Rafael use with the unknown t_1 quantity?
_____

8. How many clay balls does Rafael use with the unknown t_2 quantity?
_____

9. Look at the pattern between the two values. Write an algebraic equation showing the relationship between *t* and *c*. _____

10. Use your equation to solve for t_1. _____

11. Use your equation to solve for t_2. _____

c	t
4	6
6	9
8	12
10	15
—	—
—	—
—	—
20	t_1
50	t_2

Word Problems in the Produce Aisle

Priscilla's Produce offered the following items at the labeled costs. Mrs. Fredrickson was doing weekly shopping when several questions arose regarding the produce. Use the information from the produce aisle to solve the problems below.

lettuce	$1.29 per head	bananas	$.29 per lb.
carrots	$.59 per lb.	oranges	5-lb. bag for $3.78
beans	$1.59 per 1-lb. bag	grapefruit	$.48 per lb.
tomatoes	$.99 per lb.	grapes	$.89 per lb.
mushrooms	8-oz. container for $1.79	nectarines	$.48 per lb.
mushrooms	16-oz. container for $3.19	apples	3-lb. bag for $3.59
onions	$.67 per lb.	apples	$.89 per lb. separately
potatoes	$.33 per lb.	strawberries	$1.55 per pint

1. Mrs. Fredrickson estimates each tomato to weigh about 3/4 pound. How many tomatoes does she have if she buys 3 lbs.? _____ What is the cost? _____

2. Potatoes come in 5- and 10-lb. bags. What is the price of each bag? _____

3. Each 3-lb. bag of apples has 8 apples in it. How much does each apple weigh? _____ What is the cost per apple in the 3-lb. bag? _____

4. Assuming the individual apples weigh about the same as the apples in the bag, which is the better bargain, to buy apples loose or in bags? _____

5. Mrs. Fredrickson buys 2.5 pounds of loose apples. How much does she pay? _____

6. A large bunch of bananas has 7 bananas and weighs about 2.3 lbs. A small bunch has 4 bananas and weighs about 1.3 pounds. About how much does each banana weigh? _____ How much might Mrs. Fredrickson expect to pay for a 10-banana bunch? _____

Sylvia, the student sleuth, needs to send a secret coded message to her boss, Irvin, the investigator. Unfortunately, Sylvia only knows Irvin's progress around the United States. Before she can send the message, she must use the map information and her mathematical skills to discover his whereabouts. Use the Internet, encyclopedias, and/or atlases to help Sylvia unravel the clues below. Then label and use the map on page 44 to track the leads to discover Irvin's location. Solve the secret code Sylvia will send him at the bottom of this page.

Clues to Irvin's Location

1. Irvin's last known location was in a capital city in the southeast whose number of letters, when squared, totals 121. _____

2. From there he traveled at about a 30° angle northwest to a capital city with an even-lettered name.

   _____

3. Next he traveled north to a state who's southern line segment border is the only one that touches land. _____

4. Then he took a train due south through four states where he made an abrupt 90° turn to the west and traveled about 1,500 miles to another capital city. _____

5. Using the perpendicular crossing of the four adjacent states' borders as the vertex, he next flew to a capital city which lies 100° and about 1,000 km from the vertex. _____ (**Hint:** Perpendicular lines intersect at a 90° angle. The name of this capital city has the same number of letters as the state in which it lies.)

6. His last stop took him due east for about 2,200 miles to a city whose number of letters and the number of letters in the state it's in are factors of 42. _____

7. Where is Irvin? _____

Directions: Insert the first letters of the solutions above for numbers 1–6 into the spaces below to break the code.

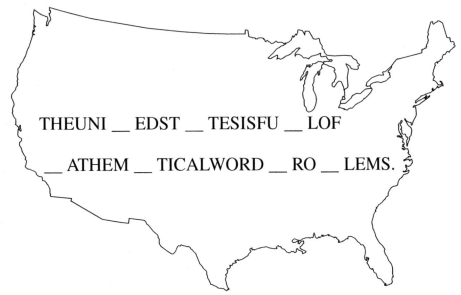

THEUNI __ EDST __ TESISFU __ LOF

__ ATHEM __ TICALWORD __ RO __ LEMS.

Use this map to label and track the clues on page 43 to discover Irvin's whereabouts.

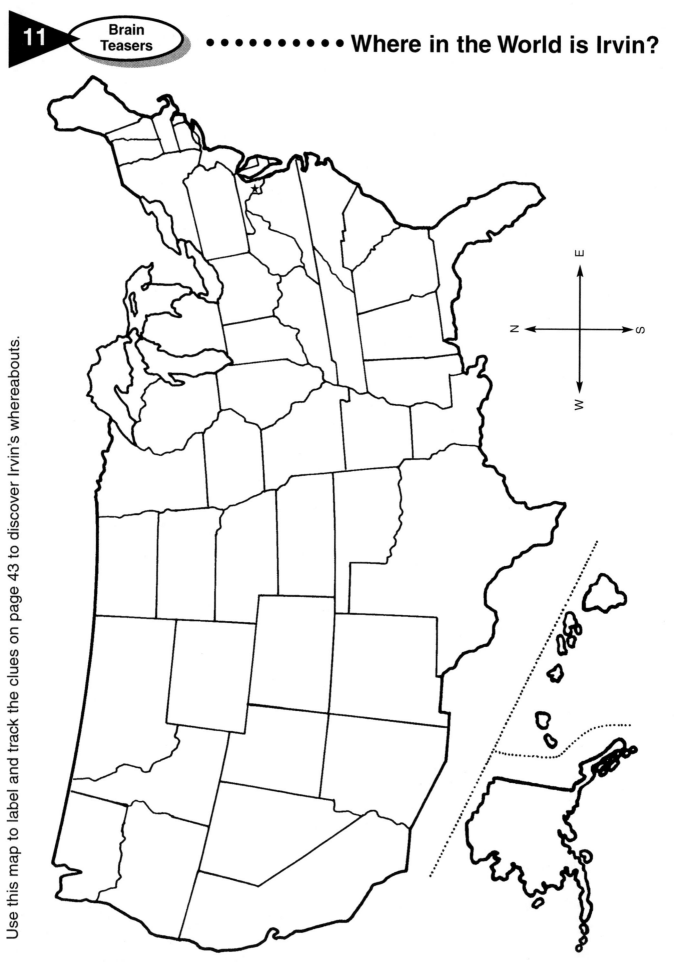

12 ▶ Technology •••••••••••••••••••••• **Internet Movie Link**

Here's your chance to go online to find out the latest movie crazes sweeping the box offices! With this information you may select any one of the following activities.

Directions:

1. Go online to *http://www.yahoo.com*

2. Click the Entertainment link, then the Movies and Film links.

3. Find the Yahoo! Movies link, or go directly to

   http://movies.yahoo.com/movies/

4. Find the list of the latest top 10 movies. List them on the lines below in order from number one to number ten.

5. Poll your family, classmates, teachers, and others to find out which movie is each person's number one choice to go see. (If they've already seen one or more of the movies listed, they may still choose one of these titles as their top choice.) Tally your findings to the right of the movie title.

6. Complete one of the activities listed below, using your data.

	Movie Title	**Tally**
1.	_____	_____
2.	_____	_____
3.	_____	_____
4.	_____	_____
5.	_____	_____
6.	_____	_____
7.	_____	_____
8.	_____	_____
9.	_____	_____
10.	_____	_____

Activities

• Use your data to write five math-related questions on the back side of this paper. Have a classmate answer the questions.

• Enter your data into a spreadsheet file. Then highlight the data to make a bar graph.

• Create a movie schedule for a six-movie complex. Use the 10 titles as the movies currently showing. Be sure to research the movies' lengths so as not to double-book any titles.

• Go online to find out how much money each movie has grossed to date. Create a graph of this information.

The word problems in this book provided the necessary information in order for you to solve the problems. But what if you needed to use a data bank available on the Internet? This activity has you integrating technology with problems you create yourself using data found on the Internet. Follow the directions to create your very own hyperlink word problems!

Directions

1. Go online to your favorite search engine. Research some sites that offer quantities, figures, or data you are interested in researching. Examples might be the depths of seas around the world, the life spans of various mammals, or the average temperatures of specific cities. Write down the Web address along with the data you are collecting.

2. Create a word problem with three to five sentences about the topic you researched. Don't include any of the data. The person answering your question will have to go online to find the appropriate information.

3. Open a multimedia computer program such as *HyperStudio*® or *Power Point*®. Create a stack to coincide with the number of sentences in your word problem.

4. Add text and graphics to each card. Link them so the user follows the sentences in the correct progression.

5. Be sure to add the Web address link site to find the necessary data.

6. Include one final card giving the answer(s). Show how you solved the problem so if the person using your stack does not have the same answer, he or she should be able to see his or her mistake.

7. Complete your hyperlink project and check all of the links, especially the one leading to the Internet site. Trade your project with another classmate. Solve each other's problems.

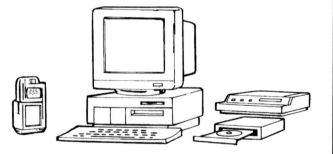

Page 6

1. length of fence, cost of materials
2. how much money he has available
3. dimensions of space in kitchen
4. divide cost of refrigerator by cubic feet it has; compare costs per cubic feet of space
5. number of pencils one of the girls has
6. Yes. Use guess and check to discover answers.
7. which is most cost/time efficient
8. No. There is not enough money left for food, hotel, sightseeing, etc.

Page 7

1. Answers will vary.
2. 8 inches by 10 inches
3. 17 girls and 13 boys
4. 82° F
5. 45
6. 5
7. 6 ways
8. 24 days

Page 8

1. No. The estimate is too high.
2. Yes. The estimate is too high.
3. No. Three dollars is more than double the single box price.
4. Yes. The estimate is reasonable (200 x 10 = 2,000).
5. Yes. The estimate is reasonable (10 mph per 20 min.).

6. No. There are too many people per car.
7. No. The estimate is reasonable ($14.31 + $25 = $39.31).
8. No. The cupcakes are much more expensive than $3 per dozen.

Page 10

1. $3.73
2. $9.45
3. $9.00
4. $14.32
5. 90; 142; 89; 150; spaghetti
6. 46 patrons
7. 855 slices
8. 542 stamps

Page 11

1. 2,500
2. 2,500
3. 500
4. 50
5. 5
6. green, yellow, red, brown
7. blue = 13; green = 18; yellow = 12; orange = 10; red = 9; brown = 15
8. 12
9. 24
10. equally likely; same number of even numbers as odd numbers
11. 24 minutes

Page 12 (*see students' charts*)

1. 8 ways
2. 21 lbs.
3. 25 lbs.
4. $8,000,000

5. $32,000,000
6. 64 blocks

Page 14

1. 450 miles
2. 375 miles
3. 75 miles
4. 27 mpg; approx 350 miles
5. 26 chaperones
6. 12 days
7. 340 votes
8. 2,260 people
9. 3,000 bags; 15,000 bags
10. 43 animals; 215 animals

Page 15

1. no
2. no
3. yes
4.–6. Answers will vary.
7. $15
8. about $7

Page 16

1. 860 miles; 1,720 miles
2. 250 beads
3. 1 inch
4. 6 inches
5. Detroit, Milwaukee, and Buffalo – 9"; Miami – 18"; Seattle – 6"
6. about 24 miles

Page 18

1. 8.5 miles
2. 270 feet
3. feet
4. 40 inches
5. 4 rolls
6. 18 weeks
7. 7 km

8. 12,000,000 m
9. 150 cm
10. 3 cm and 4 cm

Page 19

1. 3 L
2. 500 mL lemon juice, 1,000 mL water
3. the first (.5 L); 400 mL
4. 1 L or 1,000 mL
5. milliliters; A liter of medicine would be too much.
6. 25 hours
7. 5 1/2 cups
8. 16 pints
9. 80 times
10. 8 scoops

Page 20

1. tons
2. 8 oz.; Romaine
3. no; 5,000 lbs. (or 2 1/2 tons) over
4. 2 bags
5. $1,266; 10 oz.; $2,110
6. 1.89 kg
7. 37.6 g; 75.2 g; 112.8 g
8. 15 g
9. 41 g
10. 1,050 g; 700 g; 350 g

Page 22

1. 8 hr. 32 min.
2. 21 min.
3. 11 hr. 35 min.
4. 10:58 A.M.
5. 3:30 P.M.
6. 12:40 P.M.
7. 6 weeks
8. Sept. 18
9. Nov. 20
10. Oct. 18

Page 23

1. 4 hr. 55 min.
2. 190 min. or 3 hr. 10 min.
3. 1 hr. 10 min.; 4:50 P.M.
4. Jammin' Jimmies Cookies at 3 1/3 cookies per minute
5. 5 hr. 11 min.
6. $2,864; $5,728

Page 24

1. 390 hrs. or 16 days 6 hrs.
2. 30 seconds
3. about 2 months
4. 25 times
5. 2.5 hours
6. 14 months; 5 yrs. 4 mos.
7. 3 yrs. 3 mos. or 3.25 yrs.
8. 23 1/2 hours
9. 76 leap years
10. basketball, 130; rubber ball, 90; 3.9 min.

Page 26

1. 5/11
2. 1/2
3. 1 1/20 mile
4. 5/9 board
5. 1 3/4 box
6. 1/3 bag
7. 2/3 c. flour, 1/3 c. sugar
8. 12 dogs
9. 110 lbs.
10. 165 parcels

Page 27

1. cat
2. 2/3
3. hair clips

4. $.50
5. 18 to 30 = 1/3; 31 to 50 = 5/12; over 50 = 1/4
6. Fiora
7. packaging
8. packaging = 18; catchy phrases = 6
9. Ginger's
10. 1/14; 31 pages

Page 28

1. 24 people
2. 4 oz.
3. 660 ft.
4. yes, 5 hrs. 34 min.
5. 15 seconds
6. 6 1/8 yds.; 220.5 inches
7. 5/13 of the letters
8. 3 3/4; 5 7/8; 6 3/4; 8 1/2

Page 30

1. No. Check students' figures.
2. 74 polygons
3. obtuse; Check students' triangles.
4. 14 in.; 5,400 in.^{3}; 6,480 in.^{3}; 7,560 in.^{3}

Page 31

1. 65 in.
2. 22.5 ft.
3. 40" x 1"; 20" x 2"; 10" x 4"; (8" x 5")
4. 1.5 in.; 2.5 in.; 3.5 in.
5. 2,880 in.^{3}
6. Yes
7. 40 sq. ft.

Page 32

1. 90°
2. B; 1/4 mile
3. 180°
4. the Courthouse
5. 1 mile
6. 1 square mile

Page 35

1. $10.31
2. $29.25
3. $30.05
4. 36,809.6 miles
5. 25 or 26
6. 14 hrs. 40 min.

Page 36

1. $42.39
2. $116.36
3. less
4. no
5. $12.22 in change

Page 37

1. Y; Y; Y
2. Y; N, 2 oz.; N, 8 oz.
3. Y; Y; N, 1/2 oz.
4. Y; Y; Y
5. Y; Y; N, 2 oz.
6. Y; Y; N, 3
7. N, 1/2 tbsp.; N, 1 tbsp.; N, 1 1/2 tbsp.
8. N, 6 oz.; N, 14 oz.; N, 22 oz.

Page 39

1. 6^3
2. $38,000,000
3. 36,000,000 miles
4. 67,000,000 miles
5. 900,000,000 miles
6. 2,800,000,000 miles
7. 12 ft.
8. 12 ft.

9. 1,728 ft.^{3}
10. 128–256 pieces

Page 40

1. $10 - p = 4$
2. $53 + b = 105$
3. $3y = 96$
4. $100 \div t = 25$
5. $12w = 108$
6. $1,368 - d = 1,250$; $d = 118$ feet
7. $12g = 1,728$; $g = 144$ pens
8. $2s = 18$; $s = 9$ students

Page 41

1. 8
2. 12
3. 80
4. 120
5. 2
6. 3
7. 20
8. 50
9. $t = c + 1/2c$
10. 30
11. 75

Page 42

1. 4; $2.97
2. $1.65; $3.30
3. 6 oz.; $.45
4. loose
5. $2.23
6. about 5 1/4 oz.; $0.95

Page 43

1. Tallahassee
2. Little Rock
3. Michigan
4. Phoenix
5. Boise
6. Albany
7. Albany, NY; Code: The United States is full of mathematical word problems.

Page 45

Answers will vary.